About the Author

Ria Kid is a queer Afghan-American writer, artist, and a singer/songwriter for the indie-music group, Good Company. Earning a bachelor's degree in human development from the California State University, Long Beach, influenced Ria to have a more holistic perspective of the world, and prompted her to understand individuals through the same lens. She is a chronic pain survivor which sent her on a journey through a range of careers including makeup artist, wastewater project manager, audiobook narrator, etc. She currently has curated the art show, Chispa, that is an immersive art experience to indulge all the senses based on *The Muse of Manifestations*.

The Muse of Manifestations

Ria Kid

The Muse of Manifestations

Olympia Publishers
London

www.olympiapublishers.com
OLYMPIA PAPERBACK EDITION

Copyright © Ria Kid 2024

The right of Ria Kid to be identified as author of
this work has been asserted in accordance with sections 77 and 78 of
the Copyright, Designs and Patents Act 1988.

All Rights Reserved

No reproduction, copy or transmission of this publication
may be made without written permission.
No paragraph of this publication may be reproduced,
copied or transmitted save with the written permission of the publisher,
or in accordance with the provisions
of the Copyright Act 1956 (as amended).

Any person who commits any unauthorized act in relation to
this publication may be liable to criminal
prosecution and civil claims for damage.

A CIP catalogue record for this title is
available from the British Library.

ISBN: 978-1-80439-188-4

First Published in 2024

Olympia Publishers
Tallis House
2 Tallis Street
London
EC4Y 0AB

Printed in Great Britain

Dedication

Para Chispa. Siempre te he amado y siempre lo haré. Esta verdad es atemporal.
To the muse, and all the people who feel just like her.
Especially in the Afghan diaspora. We exist and it's beautiful.

Acknowledgements

If for one moment you believed in me, I know you felt my he-Art and that tiny spark of magick you felt gave me strength. If you hurt me, I am grateful for the growth I took from it. If you loved me, I am grateful to have been gifted the privilege to have felt it. If you hated me, I am grateful you taught me to be confident without a crew; to be principled without a person behind me. That the only person I ever needed was me. I have immortalized myself between these pages and I wouldn't have felt brave enough without all of you. Thank you.

The Reason

Let me proclaim
Exclaim away
Every doubt you ever had
That I was in love with you.
It would be a lie
To say this isn't a love letter
And I am tired of lying to you.

If you hate every word
At the least
Let your heart rest easy
That you have mine.

Had mine…

Just Girls

I thought you thought
We were just being girls.
When I felt home in your hands
I thought you felt skin
Friendship on fingertips
It was there but there was more
A maze of messages mapped on fingerprints.

I thought you thought
We were just being girls
When in my world
You weren't "just" anything.
Thought you could know
Without words where I was
With my fingers between yours
That worlds would never
Could never really stay
Between us.

But I didn't say
It.
I didn't say I was in love with a girl
Because you weren't "just" a girl.
You were the last and first light
At every horizon.

You were my sun with the
Skies in-between your thighs and
You embodied peace in a war of lies.
It was no liaison
It was something I prayed on.

What way could I relay what was
Really at play without
Sounding crazy?

I didn't say it because
I thought you thought
We were just being girls.
Now I understand words unsaid
Are universes undiscovered
And I plan on professing every planet of
Perfection, paused and pressed
Into my palm.

I thought you thought
We were just being girls.
We were more.

We were so much more.

Treasure

I think about you
Reading each one
Of these words
Rouge will tint your cheeks in embarrassment.

Will you fall with me?

Let me pull you through the looking glass
And nurture the blaze inside.

Will you fall through possibility with me?

Back to bathrooms of giggling bliss
Where I dreamed of lapping the magick between your thighs
And started mapping the curves of your body pushed up
Against the wall.

Be my muse, a museum of manifestation.
It felt illegal to touch you
Now I know it's because you were treasure.

Fucking treasure…

Echo

How could I tell you?
How could I tell you?
That I prayed to your smile every morning and to your skin every night?
I'm a fool of the largest sort
Not to show you that every inhale next to you put heaven
Below and if I didn't get there

I didn't care.
I didn't care.
I didn't care.
And that scared me.

Being damned was a boon
A festering freedom beneath your feet
A consecrated creed in every curve.
I crawl my way back to your curse…

Again
Again
Again
To feel every word from your mind rumble in mine.

How could I tell you?
How could I tell you?

Every crease between us I folded thinking we would both be saved
I only managed to twist myself in knots and trip at your feet
Where castigation lingers in your gaze.

I wish you would massacre me like you have murdered my peace of mind.

I'd martyr myself for a moment in your mouth again again again again again again…
To fall into you like an echo.

I keep trying to earn a place on your hit list
Hoping your smile will solidify and I could burn into ash with my lies
But I keep finding myself in closets
Prostrating at your feet.

The surrahs I whispered on your skin a singeing scar on my lips.

Me-dusa

The words she said
I fictitiously forget
Pretended not to hear
Acted unrepentant
Ghosted every dream.
Haunted every hetero.
Every pussy-paramour
Would be no more.
A countdown crisis
I can't indulge in them
In filling me up, knowing
They will never measure up
To you.

So I pour myself out instead
Emptying myself of everything
Except
Your words
That brand my blood
Stain my soul
And pump malice into mirrors.
With Perseus no nearer
The fluttering bird in my chest
Is stone already.

11:11

Under sheets of lust
My paramour is blind
To her
Incendiary effect
Amorous to my devotions
Her eyes see
My perch upon her petals as provisional
Flighty
Forging honey in the garden
Of an ailing queen.

She misunderstands
I love roses
I like daisies…
Sometimes just to destroy them

If I could drown in her dew
And inhale her into my pores
Every evening
Exhale
The apotheosis of truth
Every morning
Whispering 11:11
As a mantra on your skin
So you would know

I wished for you.

Every migration missed
Created meters of insanity
I filled with shredded daisies
And plucking my own petals.

Copper heartstrings hemorrhaging
Attempting to suture my soul
With stitches of seconds in your embrace
Whispering 11:11 behind the skin of your ear
Wishing for you.

Repent/Atone

It's impossible to resist
Carving crimson
Seductive straight lines
Into the branches of worship
Awaiting absolution.

Now

The arbor-glyphs consume me
Limbs languid
Each fib raised to the tenth power
Multiplying moments in her
Raven hurricane of refuge
Only to tumble down the
Rabbit hole.

The aroma of strawberries
Magnificence I never imagined
Could be mine.

A pandemonium of pigeons pass judgement
Their claws clinging to my nostrils
Suffocating and spewing sewage-stained statements.

I trace the tracks

Dreaming of digging out decisions
And planting them in different gardens
Editing
Until I could be enough
Until I find her.

At the center of
The labyrinth of adorations
And proclaim before
All

What has been burning on my tongue
Since sanity left with you
To kneel at your side
And picture white lace
On the plains of every power
She has over me
Trusting
I had thrown out enough thorns
To hearken Eden in her dialect.

Cream and Cinnamon

Un beso de canela y crema
Nothing could keep me warmer
I chose glass mountains
That melted beneath my feet
That burned my knees
Dripping and taciturn
When I could have been drinking
Cream and cinnamon
Memorizing every constellation
The chill bumps created
Stealing each degree
And reheating it against my lips.

I settled for *un beso*
Un beso
De canela y crema
And I dream of it on every mountain
Knowing I chose glass instead.

Lips

Crimson lips and crooning
Words skipping and soothing
Where are we?
Are we moving?
Truths are slow to stirring
Regret
Wrathful
Burning
Screaming
Stampeding regret.

Downturned carmine
Bellows of ballads
Verses of vices
Of prices paid and engrained
Splayed for the world to see
Lick these lips and call me cupid
Love needs a new face.

Obsession

My hands disagree with my decision
To write about anything but you
Our brief brush
Possessing every spare second of the day.

I am suffocating in stupidity and you aren't angry.
You don't even know I can't breathe.
You didn't know then either.
You resuscitated my soul with

Two words.

Slay me.
Maim me.
The words come so little now
All other sound has lost meaning
My rationale as vigilant as Van Gogh.
If you won't hate me
I will do it for both of us.
Death procrastinates and plays with me
The withdrawals are scathing.

It's not obvious to you I'm suffering?
I can't stop skipping the stones in my head to you.

Hey kid.

Queen

She swarms my every thought
Attacking each one until only
She
Is left.
Every individual moving piece
A memory so beautiful
It hurts
It stings
Because I know that is all I can do with them
Remember
And hurt
And yet I welcome the swarm to envelope me.
To lose myself in each one.
To find myself in each one.

Knowledge

You thought I was blowing smoke
And so I will have to live
Ruminating at the sky
Every cloud a creature of a future blundered

By my ignorance.

To not feel the sun on my face
And bask in your sunset of perfection
And know
Every mile of sky
Is as endless as you.

Submerged

I don't understand what possesses your eyes
To look into mine and submerge in mischief and magick
Under violet skies of prospect
Where moons breathe in multiples and tango
Only to show me buried treasure
Is mapped on the scalps of the knowing.

Forfeit

Even in your friendship
I am confounded.
I have no rights to you
I forfeited those long ago
But your thoughts
I yearn to know.
Staggering silences after
Slashed seconds stolen.
Not stolen.
I have no rights to you
I forfeited those long ago
But your mind
Makes madness of mine.
Murder me if you must
I just want to know
What it sees in the dark
What warning whispered
White lies
To have us break stride
When it felt some days
Like we were side by side?
I am resigned to accept your absence.
I have no rights to you
I forfeited those long ago.

No buts.

Petal Pieces

Did I rip magic off myself
Crush it
Like rose petals
Between my palms and
Blow
Them onto your flesh
The dandelion seeds pollinating
Absorbing my freckled sunlight?
Are you an illusionist with my fragrance?

Or

Were we torn from each other
Far before the soils for palms and flesh
Existed
And I am only trying to make
What was one once more?
To unify you with you
And me with me.
Were we rooted together
Before we can remember?

Stop strutting your stems in hems
Through my brain.
Its cruel enough to catalyze my karma

In compassion and caresses
That I can't keep
Anywhere
But in the past.

Mixtape Etc.

You curse me with music
I memorize
Live in every word and
Wonder
If the ballad is a disguise
And, to my demise
I missed the message
Because I believe you
Don't love me.

You can't.

After years of lying
Why would you?
Allegro or adagio
I'm unsure what beat
I'm supposed to dance to
Or if the rhythm is for me

At all.

Say something, please
Even if it's to break
What's already broken.
I'm leaning into every lyric

And losing my mind.
I missed the first
Message in melody
And I'm afraid
I've missed multiple.

The mixtapes you made me
The playlists
They play me.
I'm past the point of praying.
Please. Please.
Just tell me.

Fool

I hate you
You're perfect.
Let me ruin it all
Again, again, again
Because I need to know
If you love me too.
Sleep evades me
But stupidity stays.
I did this because
I wanted to know.
You didn't want to tell me
To protect
My senseless soul.
How is your magick
Intoxicating
After years apart?
I am drunk on you.
It's stupid and unfair.

I want to turn it off.
I can't have you.
I surround myself in relics
Of you.
I'm a fool.
So I ruin it all

Again, again, again
To save what's left of
My idiotic heart.

Dance Break

I'm tired of dancing with you
Of speaking in side-steps.
You say you will lead
But I learn everything late.
When I move forward
It's one, two steps back.
Stop spinning me in circles
With freedom between your fingers
Meeting me in dreams
In past lives
Where we partnered and
Prayed to each other in
Pirouettes and
Sex was the essence of
Presence
When we moved in motion
More n'sync than any ocean
Manifesting magick
In each mirrored act.
Turn me toward the truth
Our truth.
Tell me where this tango
Takes us.

S-Wet

I used to dream
When my heart was lonely
Of slipping into your pocket
To share all of our silences
My head humming with
Peace in the pulse.
I felt small then
A parasite preying on
Your warmth.

Now I dream of
Being every bead
Of sweat on your body.
To trace wet lines until
Exhausted with euphoria
I dare whisper cool air
On your neck.
To love with ardor
Worthy of you.

Noose

Did you think I was happier
When he put his arms around me?
That I enjoy straightjackets?
Every time you walk in
I feel my hands are tied
The noose burning
You were right
And now
Mine will never be
Around your waist
Tasting grace
On the corners of your lips.

Reciprocity

I thought I could love someone
The way you loved me
And feel just the same
Love isn't cause and effect.

P-Love-Cebos

Life is exhausting without you.
The anxiety that has haunted me
Has only been your absence.
I'll take every pill…
I take every pill.
None has ever steadied
My staggering heart
The way the smell of your hair
And the safety of your arms have.

I overdose on placebos of you
Praying my pressed pupils fail to open
But no such luck.

I guess that's my medicine to swallow.

Quake-er

I attempted to walk into your life
Tiptoeing.
You didn't tell me how loud
My footsteps had become;
That I was thundering and
Quaking
Through your world.
I wished only to make your legs tremble
The way your lips do
When they say
"I love you"
I never meant to create
Caverns;
A fissure of faults to
Climb out of.
I try to pull you out
But every time I
Step closer
The crevices create
Veins
A web to swallow us
Both.
I am terrified of
Losing you…
I am terrified of losing myself…

And the longer this goes on
The ground beneath my
Fearful feet
Crumbles.

Loyal-ties

And though my loyalty lies with the queen
She fails to see the
Flogging
I have endured just to look at her.
Most of the time I don't care.
This isn't most of the time.

Losing Game

I sip on cancerous smoke
Hoping death comes sooner.
This beautiful, tiresome life
Has exhausted me air.
How do I apologize for crimes
Forced into my fists
Waterboarding me into hurting you?

I manifested a nightmare
And I don't know how.

I hurt you…
Without doing…
Without knowing…
Without trying…

The universe is fighting me for you
And I am fighting back
And I am losing.
Will you see the difference?
Or will you think what
My nightmares show me
That I wouldn't try every way in the world
To be close to you.

How do I fuck this up
Every time
When all I'm determined to do
Is be close to you?

Hard Truths

I have ruined my life in ways that will never let her
Love me.
I made all those decisions because I thought she would never
Love me.

Are You?

I'm sorry that you lose yourself
When you're with me
That when you look into
Lifetimes in my eyes
You lose time
That I have always felt right at the
Wrong time.
I'm sorry you get careless
When you are around me
That feeling alive makes you
Forget the mundane
Pains of life
But you greet strife at your doorway
In the morning.
I'm sorry loving me has felt so free
That the world falls away and
My lips feel like the sun on your face
Only to remind you that night
Is inevitable and
You'll never let me
Hold you in it.
I'm sorry the world seems more beautiful
Sunsets more magical
When I'm lying in your arms
With your fingers tangled in mine and

The sweetness of your breath against
My neck
Knowing you may never want to know how
Breathless
You make me.
I'm sorry I always try to make you laugh
More than I make you cry because
I selfishly enjoy
Kissing your smile and not
Your tears
But you would never be that naked
With me
Fearing vulnerability.

I'm sorry. I'm sorry. I'm sorry.
Are you?
I'm sorry. I'm sorry. I'm sorry.
Are you?

Abort

Apathy has transcended anger
And, although attentive
Your affections were absent
In an abhorrent attempt to
Abort them along with me.
I was alien and atrocious
And in ample need of adorations
To aide my ailing self-assurances.

I am now only sure that I am alone.

Part 3

Part 1.
The moon is bright
The night never seems to come
Its powerful gaze
A lighthouse
And though the darkness is thick
My eyes see everything and
Know
There is hope still breathing
Near the grave of her cousins.
My love, when you are near
Ever fear feels mousey to
Losing you
When I have been waiting
For the day to come
For years.
It may be true that you haven't
Been here for very long
Yet showing your face for
A fraction of that time has beheld
A luminescence to
Dispel every fear.

Part 2.
I didn't know you'd say goodbye
In less than a year.

Stalker

It has yet to be a full day
Without your voice
And I am trembling in misery.
Dirt is still beneath my nails
From being dragged away
From you, the phantom's grip
Bruising my ankles.
The only ghost I had ever
Been afraid of was yours
Until now.
Where this new vulture
Watches me in portals
Vulnerable and
Naked in front of you.
They watched me say
What I have wanted to do
For years
Places my hands never held
And my lips couldn't reach
Destinations damned
A thousand times before
And now
Not even words can
Touch them.
This wraith will pay.

They will atone in
Hexes and heresies
Banished to the shadows
Where my compassion now lies
Melting and smoldering.
Until then
When my eyes shut
I caress every curve of your face
See the bronze of your eyes
And kiss the cinnamon of your lips.
Until then
I travel back to lakes of innocent lust
When your laugh shook my soul
The freckle sitting on the edge of your smile
Taking what's left of it.
Until then
I visit past lives with you
Trying to remember every detail
To cling to.

I'll meet you there every night
My love
Until my eyes meet yours again
I'll meet you there every night.

Rivers/Reverse

My love expands like ripples in the river
Nourishing all those who reach for it
But the ripples never reach the starting point.

Even rivers need wells of themselves to drink from.

People have made deserts of dams
Demand they learnt the tides as they have the seasons.
No one will die thirsty.

Especially not me.

Brushfire

The curve of your smirk
Leaves me weak with desire
And every time we touch
You're quick to inspire.
A paintbrush for life
You make everything brighter
My hands itch to burn
Your skin, a brushfire.
Your soul is so radiant
It bursts through the base
Leaving gems for my
Tongue to trace.
Enamored by you
I don't know what I'll do
If I can't make my way back to you.
Enraptured by you
I never want to lose
The way I am when I'm with you.

Rings

She says she loves me
That nothing is above me

Except

This

Boundary

She keeps moving
For me.

I say I need to be free
People need to be free
But please choose to be
Free with me.

I'll respect that you can leave
That you choose me
Day after day
But I didn't make this discovery
Before I let that line
Circle me
Ring me around in
Aesthetical fallacies

That time meant you couldn't leave.
That's not true though
I found you.
I am free to do.
But you don't like what I choose…

The ring was a punitive thing
Symbolic of things
Sure
That's true…
But now it's
Be happy
I love you
Be true to you.

I want you to feel that way too.
I want you to feel happy too.

Fairytales Are Still Fairytales

Once upon a time
There was a girl
Who grew to love a
Woman.

But it was complicated.

Scarface but Not

It's amazing that
LOVE
Can be so
POWERFUL
It makes you pray for
DEATH.

5

Five years.
Five years of fallen promises
Foolish conversations and
Fated dates.
Five years.
Five years of forget-me-nots
That were forget-me-always
And fortunes unmade.
Five years.
Five years of feeling fastened
To this fork in the road
Focusing on frames to fit in.
Five fucking years
And when I accepted aloneness
And my footsteps inflamed your fears
I am worth fighting for.
How can I forget five years
Of forgetting me?
How can I forget five years
Without family or friends
Or love?

For you, I offered everything.
For me, I am everything now.

I won't forget myself again.

Please, Come In

I will always remember your love
Couldn't walk through my front door
Not when sick
Not when well
Because discomfort was louder in your ears.
I won't remember your embrace
While I lose life in droplets.
When I whisper goodbyes
I'll wish for your face
Only to feel the cold of mine.

I was never treasure enough for you to love.

Forget-Me-Knots

Why can't I forget you?
Can't wish I'd never met you.
Your silence is deafening
Space feels like pretending
We don't know exactly what
This is.
Why can't I forget you
When you've forgotten me
And I only get to see you in
My dreams?
Why can't I forget you
When your cruelty is clear?
Understandable
You don't want to
Be here.

Why
Why
Why

Can't I forget
You?

I won't get over it.
I don't want to move on.

I'll do what I have to
If you decide I'm too much
And still.

Now
Always
Again

I can't forget
You.

Leftovers

I settle for a stick figure
Scribbled on a scrap
To spend sunsets with
Your smile
And the space
Between your fingers
Is the solace I'm searching for.

I may laugh like a hyena
But scraps are not what I am seeking.

Bitter

You took yourself away in a day.
I took myself back in pieces
And now I see that bitterness
Tastes sweeter on your tongue
Than honesty.

Just Say the Word

I've proclaimed
Exclaimed my love
And you left empty airs
Of confusion
Clouds full of
Fables.

I didn't lie.

I can see in your eyes
There's doubt
And I don't understand
When I've planned and told you
Over and over again
Lifetimes with you is what
I have always wanted.
That if you wished
I would've granted

Anything.
Anything.
Anything.

Six-Sided Seductress

Six-sided seductress
Says nothing and still
I see her
Screaming my name
Sliding my fingers
Between her legs
Saying "*te amo*"
Again and again.

Her whispers haunt
My every moment.

Six-sided seductress
Says we need space
I didn't know we'd be
Lightyears away
That we'd orbit
And our lips would never meet
Not even to say
Good morning.

And I understand
She saw me surrender
Myself.
My self.

It was messy.

But a spills insight
Could spark coherence
Much quicker than
Simple steps ever could.
See me for the solid lover
I am now.

I miss you, six-sided seductress.
Please say something sweet again.
Sighs stay heavy
With your memory.
I want to see you again.

Please say you'll stay
Six-sided seductress.
I promise I am worth
The wait.
I promise
I am
Worth
The wait.

Hugo's Heartache

Miss St. James
I know you love me.
I know you'll never stop thinking
Of me.
Miss St. James
Let's not waste time.
I feel like I've been waiting
All my life.
Miss St. James
Don't ignore the urge.
We both know you want me
In your bush.
Miss St. James
Don't make me lie.
Say you want to be friends
With your lips on mine.

From Earth With Love

How can I be sad when the world
Is full of wonder I have yet to
Discover
I've mined for love and
Treasured jewels between the thighs
Of lies
And now I make love
To the sunrise and
She
She always cums.
She rises and with it
So do the corners of my lips.
How can I be sad when the world
Is full of wonder and I can find
A lover
When the sun kisses saltwater
In the sunset and
He
He always cums.
He tucks me into bed and
Drains every pain of the day
In his eyes.

Four-Letter Love

It's impossible to reach you
When I measure my love for you
In each second I have
To stare into your face
Each minute with your warmth
Next to me
Yet you measure your love for me
By pennies in each pocket.
A finite figure
You run out of it too often
And when you are bankrupt
Are hollow of hearts for me
You pull one from behind your ear
And offer it to a magician
His cloak full of them.
I didn't know you traded mine
One I had stashed in secret
And gilded in guilt.
I didn't know your love for me
Was a four-letter word.

Cash.

The Truth Is in the Type-Writer

I am
I am
I am
So exhausted of the cycle of
Disappointments and callous caresses
Only to find cracks on the surface of your
Fabled love.

We don't agree on the last.
We don't agree on much.

I am
I am
I am
Tired of settling for pebbles
When I deserve ponds of affections
For sacrifices unsung.

I can't
I can't
I can't
Suck oxygen through a straw
Indefinitely for your comfort with
Your fingers blistering my neck.

Instead of suffering your solemn stare
And empty words
Attempting aide with failed intent
Loose stitching and blind surgeon
I cement my soul into sentences
Ingraining my veracity this time
And every time after.
A type-O typewriter
Screaming truth into existence.

There is no escape for you.

What will you say when they ask you about this?
What flamboyant excuse is waiting
This time
To deny every tear that escaped
Sliding towards terminal refuge?

Oh, how I wish I could join them.

To flee this cavernous confinement
And have limbs languidly erupt in
The April sun
Spurting scarlet secrets through every seam
Staining your every image of
Me.

Freckles

A creature of the night
I cocoon myself in
A shell of security to
Protect my wounded worth.
Trapped
I explosively emerge
Expanding my wings
As if to embrace the sky.

I rub the sleep from my eyes
As the setting sun
Sighs and succumbs to
The ebony tapestry of night
I mine for the jewels
The freckles of Sol
To invent a luminosity
Original to me.
I forget that what made it
Unique
At all
Was that I created it.

Chests

I hid in leather-bound treasure chests
Searching for a whispered promiseland
Where I could hear my name without flinching.
A score of years have passed
Since I had the first taste of gold between my fingers and still
I hear the wind
Calling me
Telling me the land is near and the journey's end is in sight.

I thought that clarity had escaped me
I thought breaking myself into pieces
Buried in every chest
Could be another way to find my land
But it was too hard to

Keep

Everything

Together

When I found tiger's eye and onyx
On the surface of the only land that matters.
Rubies hid in the valleys

And the mountains tempt at every point.

The promised-place has always been mine.

I never noticed the miniature sign
Covered in thousands of flowers
Captured only by memory.

I have been here for years and yet
Never realized
I have always been here.

Welcome to belonging.
Population: 01

Pink Glasses

Maybe we'll live together
Make café de olla in the morning
And go on walks in the morning dew.
Maybe we'll have breakfast
Chilaquiles and for you
Huevos divorciados
Then slide under white covers of comfort
And ecstasy before the world

Wakes up.

Maybe.
Maybe we'll only say maybe
Manifest only more maybes
And go back to bumping into each other.

Maybe I only said maybe
Because I thought we'd make magic and maybe you'd
Love me.
Maybe you'd see our ruffled sheets
Crème brulée as sweet as your skin
And us kissing before every constellation.

Maybe you'd see five shades of brown
When you look into

My eyes
And understand that I see
Everything
In yours.

Maybe you'd see I'm home with you
Think about growing old with you
Hoping
You aren't wearing pink glasses
See, the only thing
Rose-toned
Are my lips.

Even If I wanted

The fates have decided
That I'm not invited
To sit by your side
Pray to call you my wife.
Every time I make plans
They blunder them badly…
Make me look mad
Like I'm thinking grandly.

But I know
I know the truth.
I know.
That someone
Something
Has kept me from
You.

But I'm tired
Of losing keys
Of losing sleep
Of losing peace
Of mind
Having someone follow me
Something rob
Me…
What's left except to
Take my life?

Pretender

"I don't know"
Isn't an answer.
I know
I said it too
But not to you.
Not for you.

My mind is made up and
Manifesting you daily because
I don't want to live with maybes.

And I know that
You love me.

So when I won't waste time without you
Worry when what-if wishes will
Come true
I'll love, and love again
And then

I'll love you again.

My mastery lies as a marksman of
Mending.
And I still know that

You're pretending.
It's why you try so hard to
Forget me
When it's truly an
Impossibility.

Stop fighting what we should be
When you know
And I know

It'll always be me.
It has always been me.
It will always be me.

Coffee Break

I wonder about the coffee shop.
I know we talked about nineteen
But we were such young things.
I wonder more about the coffee shop.

I wonder when I put my heart out
Told you I loved you then
And maybe now…
You slid the plate back toward me
As if declining bread.

You said I didn't try hard
Enough.
You said I should have
Pushed harder.

I don't force dessert on people
Who don't enjoy sweets
And I don't force feelings to
Fly from your mouth
But to say I didn't try hard
Enough, well
That just not true.

I wonder if in that coffee shop

You had said what you actually felt.
I wonder what life would've been
If we had made love a thousand times
Then, would anything be
Different?

I'm not saying you didn't
Show me you cared.

I'm saying
I've come to be braver than
You.
I wonder about the coffee shop
If you had held my hand
If that spark would have burned as bright
Or still would have burnt them.

All I'd hoped was that you would say
"I do too. I love you too."

Blue

You brand me a whore
When I don't think you remember
Your voice telling me
Everything you wanted to do
In blue.

We weren't in a solid place
But I wasn't concerned
I missed your face
Your lips, your smile
Your everything
I got too excited and then
Things changed.

I would never force myself
On you.
I would never disrespect
That truth.
What I wanted was to
Kiss you
In blue
Because I only thought
About kissing you
In blue.

It's hard to think of anyone else
When your voice in my ear
Had been driving in my backseat
And when I sit
In blue
I think of what you said
You wanted to do
And I don't want to kiss
Anyone but you
In the front seat
Or the backseat
Of blue.

Who's the Muse?

Who's the muse?

I called you
My queen
You called me
Your princess
Lording over me
Is not what I thought
You meant.

Who's the muse?

Cruel queens
Melt quickly
And princesses
Procure their power.
Pride is a putrid thing
My queen
And yours is palpable.

I made you mine but
I can un-make you.
I am a muse myself.
And though your absence
Is felt

I care little.

A queen
A muse, of magick
Is me
More deserving of
Love than
Anybody.

Between the Sheets

I miss your car crawling up the street
And sitting in your passenger seat
Having your hands pull my hair
Your fingers in my mouth never play fair
All I can do is suck and stare
The frosting between my thighs is sweet
And I know how much you love to eat
My tits are served at your table this week
And next will be cake between the sheets

Candied kisses
Keep them cumming
Repeat
Licking frosting off our fingers
Is our favorite treat
We both have our cake and eat it too
In between the sheets.

Rooted Together

Whisper lyrics on my lips
Like a sin
I'd do anything to taste you
Again
Read mine and between
The lines
You'll see my love
Never lies.
It's pure Magick and that
Never dies.
Lick my lips again and
Know
The taste of me will
Never go.
I'll always be on your
Bottom lip
And everytime you
Take a sip
Life is perverted with
My grip
On your mind
Reminding you
Unconditionally
Having love like mine is to
Live in Truth

And what better way
To Love
Than to love from
The root.